American Bullfrogs Invade Swamps and Ponds

By Susan H. Gray

21st Century
Junior Library

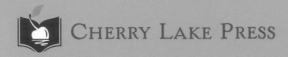

Published in the United States of America by Cherry Lake Publishing Group
Ann Arbor, Michigan
www.cherrylakepublishing.com

Reading Adviser: Beth Walker Gambro, MS, Ed., Reading Consultant, Yorkville, IL
Book Designer: Melinda Millward

Photo Credits: © Dwayne Towles/Shutterstock.com, cover; © Chris Hill/Shutterstock.com, 4;
© Mircea Costina/Shutterstock.com, 6; © Tracy Riddell Photography/Shutterstock.com, 8;
© feathercollector/Shutterstock.com, 10; © Natalia Kuzmina/Shutterstock.com, 12; © 4Max/
Shutterstock.com, 14; © Eric Isselee/Shutterstock.com, 16; © Tau5/Shutterstock.com, 18;
© Christian Ouellet/Shutterstock.com, 20

Cherry Lake Press is an imprint of Cherry Lake Publishing Group.
Library of Congress Cataloging-in-Publication Data

Names: Gray, Susan Heinrichs, author.
Title: American bullfrogs invade swamps and ponds / by Susan H. Gray.
Description: Ann Arbor, Michigan : Cherry Lake Publishing, 2021. | Series:
    Invasive species science : tracking and controlling | Includes index. | Audience: Grades 2-3
Identifiers: LCCN 2021004943 (print) | LCCN 2021004944 (ebook) | ISBN 9781534187047
    (hardcover) | ISBN 9781534188440 (paperback) | ISBN 9781534189843 (pdf) |
    ISBN 9781534191242 (ebook)
Subjects: LCSH: Bullfrog—Control—Juvenile literature. | Introduced amphibians—Juvenile literature. |
    Invasive species—Control—Juvenile literature.
Classification: LCC QL668.E27 G735 2021 (print) | LCC QL668.E27 (ebook) | DDC 597.8/92—dc23
LC record available at https://lccn.loc.gov/2021004943
LC ebook record available at https://lccn.loc.gov/2021004944

Cherry Lake Publishing Group would like to acknowledge the work of the Partnership for 21st
Century Learning, a Network of Battelle for Kids. Please visit http://www.battelleforkids.org/
networks/p21 for more information.

Printed in the United States of America
Corporate Graphics

CONTENTS

Frogs have vocal sacs that fill with air. It helps make their calls louder!

Bullfrog Songs

Rum, rum, rum, ruh-ruh-ruh, rum.
Everyone leaned closer to the speaker.

"I knew it! Bullfrogs at the campground pond!" one of the park workers cried. The young woman had spent weeks in a national park. She'd been placing sound recorders where she thought American bullfrogs lived. The devices were called song meters.

At one time, American bullfrogs only lived in the eastern United States.

The woman was part of a team that worked in **Yosemite** National Park in California. Their job was to find out where American bullfrogs lived. The frog was an **invasive species** at the park.

As large **predators**, bullfrogs ate crickets, birds, fish, and snakes. In some places, **prey** species were disappearing. The Yosemite team wanted to change that.

Look!

Look at some pictures of American bullfrogs. Why do you think people might have a hard time finding them by sight?

American bullfrogs are the largest frogs in North America.

Bullfrogs Travel the World

Farmers and gardeners have used bullfrogs to control insect pests. In many places, people have **imported** bullfrogs to raise them.

Make a Guess!

For what other reasons might people import invasive species?

American bullfrogs can lay up to 20,000 eggs at a time.

In their native home, the frogs are not a problem. Alligators, water snakes, and snapping turtles prey on them. Fish feed on the **tadpoles**. But in their adopted homes, bullfrog adults have few enemies. And tadpoles are safe too. Fish don't like their taste.

American bullfrogs can live up to 10 years. They may travel for miles, just moving from pond to pond. Once the bullfrogs arrive, it's difficult to clear them out.

American bullfrogs are able to blend in well with their environment.

The Yosemite Plan

Usually, years pass before people realize an animal has invaded. Native species begin to disappear. Scientists look into the matter. Eventually, they identify the invading species.

That's when wildlife experts jump into action. They educate the public about the troublesome species. They write articles about the invaders. They explain all the problems the invasive species is causing.

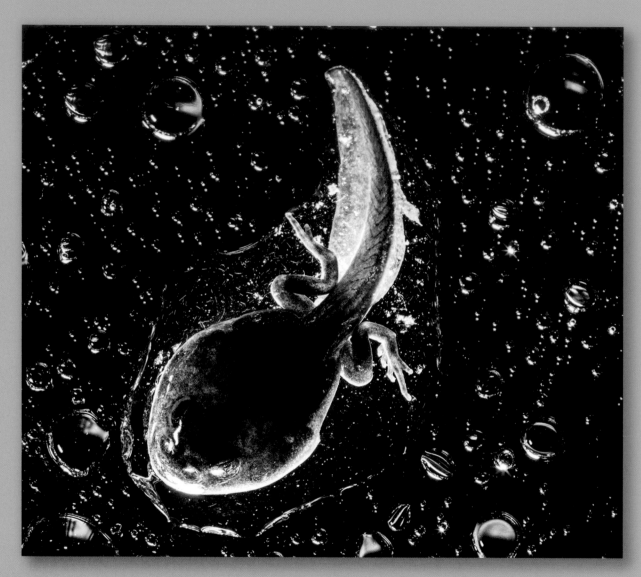

Bullfrogs spend about 14 months as tadpoles
before they mature into frogs.

In some countries, they encourage people to hunt American bullfrogs. In Europe, they helped pass laws against bullfrog imports. In the United States, Santa Cruz, California, banned all bullfrog pets, sales, and releases.

Elsewhere in California, a bigger plan was at work. This plan went after frog eggs, tadpoles, and adults. It became the first successful large-scale removal.

Think!

How could wildlife experts use social media to educate people about invasive species?

Bullfrogs are identified by their distinct golden eyes.

The plan unfolded in a valley in Yosemite National Park. They hunted the frogs and removed their egg masses. The team strained ponds to clear out tadpoles.

These people didn't want to remove *most* bullfrogs. They hoped to remove all bullfrogs. So they used special methods to find every last one. For one thing, they set up song meters. These devices recorded bullfrog songs. The recordings told workers where bullfrogs still lived. Next, the frog hunters went high-tech. They began looking for bullfrog DNA.

If scientists find bullfrog DNA in the water, they know one is nearby.

The Plan Works

DNA is a large **molecule** that exists in the cells of all living things. Bullfrog skin cells contain bullfrog DNA. Those cells are shed when a frog or tadpole swims.

Ask Questions!

What other animals might leave their DNA in water?

American bullfrogs are in at least 40 countries.

The park workers did a great job. In 2012, they removed the last bullfrog egg mass. In 2013, they scooped out the last tadpoles. Workers continued to watch for bullfrogs. And now, it seems the frogs are finally gone.

Park employees, scientists, and wildlife experts worked together. They used many methods to find the bullfrogs. Their work covered a huge area. This effort is a great success story. It shows how a good plan and hard work pay off.

GLOSSARY

imported (im-PORT-ihd) brought in from another place

invasive (in-VAY-sihv) not native, but entering by force or by accident and spreading quickly

molecule (MAHL-uh-kyool) a very small compound made up of atoms

predators (PREH-duh-turz) animals that hunt and eat other animals

prey (PRAY) animals that are hunted and eaten by other animals

species (SPEE-sheez) a particular kind of plant or animal

tadpoles (TAD-polz) young, immature stages of frogs and toads

Yosemite (yo-SEH-muh-tee) a valley and national park in California

FIND OUT MORE

BOOKS

Batten, Mary. *Aliens from Earth: When Animals and Plants Invade Other Ecosystems*. Atlanta, GA: Peachtree Publishers, Ltd., 2016.

Gray, Susan H. *Bullfrog*. Ann Arbor, MI: Cherry Lake Publishing, 2009.

Spilsbury, Richard. *Invasive Reptile and Amphibian Species*. New York, NY: PowerKids Press, 2015.

WEBSITES

BioKids—American Bullfrog
http://www.biokids.umich.edu/critters/Lithobates_catesbeianus
Read here about how the frogs live, communicate, and avoid their enemies.

National Geographic Kids—American Bullfrog
https://kids.nationalgeographic.com/animals/amphibians/facts/american-bullfrog
Learn how bullfrogs hunt and how they survive cold weather.

National Wildlife Federation—Bullfrog
https://www.nwf.org/~/media/PDFS/Garden-For-Wildlife/Kids-GFW/Bullfrogs.pdf
This site has a great printout with many bullfrog facts.

INDEX

ABOUT THE AUTHOR

Susan H. Gray has a master's degree in zoology. She has written more than 180 reference books for children and especially loves writing about animals. Susan lives in Cabot, Arkansas, with her husband, Michael, and many pets.